Made in United States
Orlando, FL
08 April 2024

45580554R00061